The Way of the Cross in Times of Illness

The Way of the Cross in Times of Illness

Elizabeth Thecla Mauro

LITURGICAL PRESS
Collegeville, Minnesota

www.litpress.org

1	2	3	4	5	6	7	8

Library of Congress Cataloging-in-Publication Data

Mauro, Elizabeth Thecla.
   The way of the cross in times of illness / Elizabeth Thecla Mauro.
      p. cm.
   ISBN 0-8146-2969-5 (pbk. : alk. paper)
  1. Sick—Prayer-books and devotions—English. 2. Catholic Church—Prayer-books and devotions—English. I. Title.
   BX2373.S5M335 2004
   232.96—dc22

2003019557

". . . that in all things God may be glorified."

1 Peter 4:11 (NAB)

The Way of the Cross is an ancient devotion of the Church which has been used for centuries to bring the believer into deeper union with the Passion of Jesus Christ, using words, prayer, imagery, and visual aids to effectively join Jesus on his walk to Calvary.

This contemporary version of the Stations is written in the hope that, in these meditations, people undergoing evaluation and treatment for physical or emotional illness may find companionship, understanding, and even, with the help of God, healing.

My prayer is that any who use these Stations will find comfort and sustaining courage in the faithful promise of Christ that he will be with us to the end. Please pray for me, also.

Elizabeth Thecla Mauro, Obl.O.S.B.

July 2003

Opening Prayer

O Christ,
You healed the deaf with a touch and a word,
"Ephphatha! Be opened."
As I open this meditation, let me be opened to you.

Let me be opened to your love,
let me be opened to your healing.

Let me be opened to your voice
and to every prompting of the Holy Spirit,
as we walk this road together. Amen.

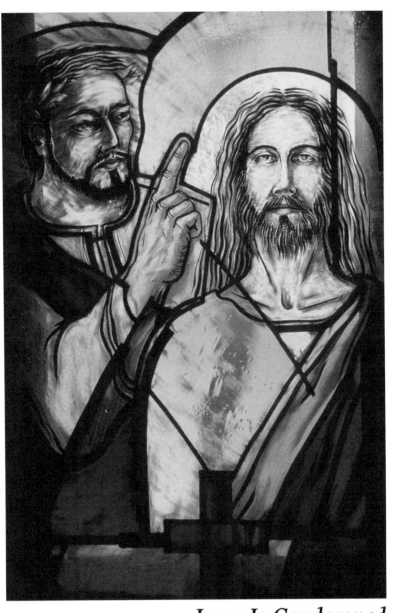

*Jesus Is Condemned
to Death*

1

*J*esus, when you stood before Pilate and received the sentence of death, you were utterly alone, abandoned by your apostles, and rejected by the crowd.

Yet you faced your fate with courage and acceptance.

Always, in every step of life, we are faced with the possibility of death—death of the body, death of the spirit, death of hope. Even when we have friends and family to turn to, ultimately we make our most difficult journeys alone. Others may sympathize and even empathize, but one person can never fully enter into another's heart of fear or pain.

Now, as I await the evaluations and recommendation of others—of medical workers, therapists, and counselors—I remember your acceptance of Pilate's decree. I don't know what lies ahead or what tomorrow will offer or take away, and I admit to my fully human fear. Give me courage and a sense of your companionship and support in this journey.

Though you had to face your walk alone, and with a certain outcome, I invite you to walk with me on this path, toward an outcome still unknown.

Do not be afraid, for I am with you; stop being anxious and watchful, for I am your God. I give you strength, I bring you help, I uphold you with my victorious right hand.

Isaiah 41:10 (JB)

2   *Jesus Bears His Cross*

*J*esus, when they handed you the cross that was to be your final oblation, your final act of offering and obedience, you were already weakened by the earlier sufferings and abuses heaped on you by others. Yet you bore your cross with extraordinary bravery and dignity. You took onto your already beaten and bruised shoulders the heavy and cumbersome wood, and you bore it.

Perhaps you even astonished and surprised some who had expected you to be too weak to receive, and to sustain, your cross.

As I face heavier burdens, heavier fears, the seemingly insurmountable weight of my own cross, I know you are with me. Having walked this path before, you will guide me, if only I keep my eyes on you.

Grant that I too may bring dignity, bravery, and strength to what I bear.

With the help of your grace, perhaps I can surprise and astonish those who think of *me* as too weak, or too fearful, to go forward.

I *will* go forward, with you, to further glorify your name.

Christ, help me to carry this.

I will instruct you, and teach you the way to go;
I will watch over you and be your adviser.

Psalm 32:8 (JB)

3   *Jesus Falls the First Time*

*W*hy do we always assume that this first fall came from your weariness and physical pain? Could you have fallen in fear? You, Jesus, who are both God and human, you understand how fear and anxiety can paralyze the will, paralyze the strength of the body, and sometimes paralyze even the strength of the spirit.

I admit that there are times when I am overtaken with fear, and I feel unable to move, to think, to pray—even to *breathe*. This fear brings with it a weariness that defies description and snatches away the small pockets of peace I am seeking in my life.

So, I fall now with you, Jesus, prostrated in fear, knowing that I must rise and go on. My face is dirty; I am gasping through the dust of the road.

But I get up with you. I breathe in deeply, and breathe out. With you, I move slowly forward.

Yahweh, I called on your name from the deep pit. You heard me crying, "Do not close your ear to my prayer." You came near that day when I called to you; you said: "Do not be afraid."

Lamentations 3:55-57 (JB)

 Jesus Meets His Mother

How helpless Mary must have felt, Jesus, seeing you in your terrible agony. When you encountered your mother on your journey, how your heart must have broken with the need to comfort her, to tell her that all would be well.

And Mary, as your mother, must have been dying inside to see you in such pain, knowing that she was helpless to do anything but remain by your side.

My family and my friends, the people I love, know something of Mary's despair. They feel helpless, angry, frustrated. They want to make my trouble "go away" and they cannot, but they are with me.

As for me, I know something of your heartbreak, because I can see those I love living with questions. I can love them in their pain, but I cannot simply step off of this path and stop this process, just as you could not, for my sake, stop your walk.

Help me to comfort them by staying faithful to you. Help me to say to those I love, "Be not afraid; all will be well," and to take heart from their company.

The angel replied,
"I will complete the journey with [your child].
Do not be afraid. On the journey outward all will
be well; on the journey back all will be well;
the road is safe."

Tobit 5:20 (JB)

5 *Jesus Is Helped by Simon*

*J*esus, we don't know much about your helper, Simon. We know he was a country man walking by, and that he was himself the father of two sons. We hear that he was "enlisted as he passed by," but might he not have been called over because of his interest?

Perhaps, seeing you struggling, he thought of how grateful he would be to anyone who would help his sons, were they in trouble.

Perhaps he saw the exchange of looks between you and your mother, and knew he must help.

All we know is this: a stranger took part of your burden and made it his own, walking with you, surrounded by the jeering, the curious, the helpless, the indifferent. He lightened the load so that you might maintain your dignity. You could feel the relief in your body, in your back, and in your knees.

How grateful you must have been for this help.

Help me to show gratitude and appreciation to the people who are helping me pastorally, physically, and emotionally. Like Simon, they are generous in their help.

Like you, let me never be outdone in generosity of spirit.

They that hope in the LORD will renew their strength,
*   they will soar as with eagles' wings;*
They will run and not grow weary,
*   walk and not grow faint. . . .*
One [person] helps another,
*   one says to the other, "Keep on!"*

Isaiah 40:31; 41:6 (NAB)

6

Jesus Meets Veronica

The tradition handed down to us teaches that during your journey a woman broke from the crowd of onlookers and brought you a small measure of comfort, wiping your bruised and bloody face. Who was this person? Some say she was the hemorrhagic woman who was cured when she touched your robes (Mark 5:29).

We're told that in gratitude for her kindness you made a gift to her, imprinting your face upon her veil. Over time, with veneration, the *vera icon,* or *true image*, came to be called "Veronica's Veil."

Although there are tales of this icon traveling as far as Rome, we may never know for certain if such a prize existed. Perhaps it doesn't matter. The story itself reminds us that we are often the beneficiaries of humble, simple consolations—by a nurse who bathes a feverish brow, a stranger who stops to give a compliment, a neighbor who brings refreshment at an unexpected moment.

I, too, have been shown kindness by strangers and by people on the periphery—those who reside on the crowded edge of my senses.

Make me more aware of, and more grateful for, the small, loving kindnesses shown to me, Jesus. When someone has been a blessing to me, help me remember to bless them in return. Help me to be more aware of the little things that come my way and keep me going, so that I might be more mindful of my own chances to do something small and good. Help me to do as Mother Teresa said, "Do small things with great love."

I give you a new commandment: love one another; just as I have loved you, you also must love one another. By this love you have for one another, everyone will know that you are my disciples.

John 13:34-35 (JB)

7 _Jesus Falls a Second Time_

*J*esus, I try to keep moving forward through what can seem like impassable mountains. Even with the support of others, I sometimes feel lonely and isolated. When those feelings surface, I fall. I lose hope, I lash out at the very people I want to keep nearest to me. I lose my temper, I lose my strength, and sometimes it seems like I lose my very will.

Yet, I know I must move on.

I wonder how it was for you in this second fall. Did you close your eyes and think, "Why won't they just let me die? Why must I get up, for what purpose must I endure this journey?"

But you did get up. Did you perhaps understand that your suffering transcended your humanity, that it went beyond the immediacy of your pain in order to serve something greater than your own wishes?

Were you simply "fulfilling your destiny" or were you showing us that life must be embraced in all of its forms, in shadow and in light, in order to be lived with a fullness of purpose?

It is a mystery to me, sometimes, why you wouldn't simply lash out and unleash the power of your tongue, verbally striking out at those around you. But you did not.

Help me, Lord. Help me overturn my own instincts to "strike out" at those around me. Help me find the key to this mystery and embrace my life in all of its forms, in its shadows, and in its light.

For it is not as if we had a high priest who was incapable of feeling our weaknesses with us; but we have one who has been tempted in every way that we are, though he is without sin.

Hebrews 4:15 (JB)

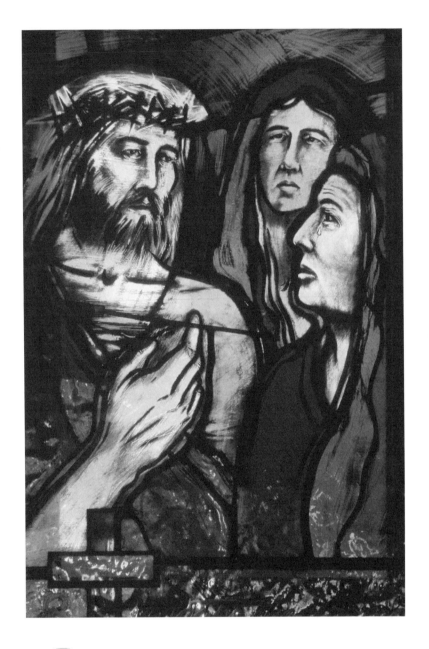

8 *Jesus Speaks to the Women*

*J*esus , your words to the women of Jerusalem always take me aback: "Weep not for me, but for yourselves and for your children." And why did you give this warning: "If these things happen when the wood is green, what will happen when it is dry?"

When times are good and the world seems green and full of promise, even then my faith has not always been all it could be. My surrender has been incomplete.

When times are dry and feelings of despair and isolation are overwhelming, I call to you. I know that I should trust, but I also realize that with trust must come acceptance, and acceptance is *hard*.

To surrender and to trust—difficult things. How totally must I surrender to your protection? How deep is your mercy? How wide and sure is your embrace? As wide as a lifetime? As sure as a wooden cross?

Help me, Jesus, to surrender to your embrace and your help with my own arms flung wide open, regretting my self-centeredness and my own human folly to think that I could travel without your lead.

Give me the gift of faith, Lord, renewed, refreshed, and green, as your psalmist promised.

> *[A person who delights in the law of the LORD]*
> *is like a tree*
> *planted near running water,*
> *That yields its fruit in due season,*
> *and whose leaves never fade.*
>
> Psalm 1:3 (NAB) 1970

9   *Jesus Falls a Third Time*

*J*esus, did you feel only weariness in this third fall, or did you also succumb to the temptation to despair, to give feeling to that enemy of hope?

Sometimes I despair too. I suppose it's only human to think that "there can be no good end to this—there can be no good gained in these painful and sad circumstances."

And yet, isn't that precisely what you were teaching me on this journey? That no matter how bleak things look, no matter what lies immediately ahead, we will find, as we move forward, that all things work for the glory of God? That peace comes in surprising ways, that some kinds of death can bring about some kinds of healing, that redemption and fullness of mercy are always, continually, being offered?

As I acknowledge my own exhaustion within my life and circumstances, I am wondering what greater purpose is being served here. How might I be helping to bring about your reign in my own small life, in my own weary but not despairing heart?

I know that I have been created by love, and that my creation serves a purpose.

O, help me, Jesus, to be attuned to what God wants of me, that I might understand my own role in this world, and in God's plan.

The life and death of each of us has its influence on others; if we live, we live for the Lord; and if we die, we die for the Lord, so that alive or dead we belong to the Lord.

Romans 14:7-9 (JB)

Jesus Is Stripped
of His Garments

10

When they stripped you, Jesus, the wounds on your back were torn open and bled anew. You were stripped beyond mere nakedness, down to your very blood, and all were invited to look.

Did they understand that they beheld the living blood of redemption?

Being stripped naked, bleeding in public—these can be metaphors for so many of our life circumstances. To be in a hospital and "publicly" stripped and bled; to face a public legal action that exposes us in a raw, painful manner; to make a mistake in front of the world: thus are we humiliated.

It's the stuff of our lives in good times and in bad, this stripping of our garments, of our modesty, our protective layer. But it is even more so for me, now, in the circumstances of this day. I look to you, Jesus, and remember that they stripped you, too.

You understand the depths of my vulnerability as no other can. But your love for me is deeper than even my deepest fears. I stand beside you, Jesus, and look only at you.

I lift up my soul
to my God.
In you I trust; do not let me be disgraced;
  do not let my enemies gloat over me.
No one is disgraced who waits for you, . . .

Psalm 25:1-3 (NAB)

11 Jesus Is Nailed to the Cross

*P*erhaps by the time you were laid on the wood of the cross, your day-long sufferings had numbed you to the pain of spikes being hammered into your flesh. Perhaps your eyes were closed and so you missed the sight of the mallet falling.

Perhaps the horror of your crucifixion is just so awful to contemplate that I prefer to think of you as being in a pain-induced stupor, unaware of these agonies as they occurred. To imagine you lucid and comprehending is too terrible. How does one find comfort in these images of torture?

And yet, things have been hammered into me, too. Hard truths I don't always want to see, knowledge of my own failings and sins, injury I have inflicted on others, or myself, or both.

There is pain in body, pain in mind, a genuine sickness of spirit that has caused me to look away rather than see the mallet that bears the consequences of my own follies and faults. But I am aware and lucid. I know that I have sinned in my life. I know the pain by which my redemption was won.

The hard truths and realities pierce me, Jesus, but *you are with me,* sharing the blows. I know that by facing these things I am living with you in a place of truth.

I know I will be free.

Gracious is the L*ORD* *and just;*
     yes, our God is merciful.
The L*ORD* *keeps the little ones;*
     I was brought low, and he saved me.
Return, O my soul, to your tranquility,
     the L*ORD* *has been good to you. . . .*
I shall walk before the L*ORD*
     in the lands of the living.

Psalm 116:5-7; 9 (NAB) 1970

12   *Jesus Dies on the Cross*

*W*hile you were dying, the crowd was jeering, "Save yourself."

We live in a "save yourself" society, a culture of self-help. Wherever we turn, we are told, "Do what is best for you." The theme of thousands of self-help books seems to be "Save yourself! Make yourself happy and you'll live more happily with others." And that's not completely wrong, but is it completely right?

Certainly, if I work toward my own happiness, I will live more fully. But does happiness and contentment lie in getting precisely what I want? Too often the concept of self-help becomes distorted and extreme. We come in danger of thinking always and only of ourselves and our "needs" without fully considering the "needs" of others.

We're not comfortable these days with the idea of sacrifice, of putting another's well-being before our own, but today I am ready to be a little bit radical. I don't want illusions or escape; they won't help me to live honestly or contentedly on this very day. Rather, I wish to look out from my pain and see where my suffering might lead. We all suffer. No one has yet been born who has not had to endure, and grow from, a time of crisis.

Today, I join my troubles to the troubles and pains of all my brothers and sisters, to the pain of your mother, Mary, who had to endure the brutal death of her beloved child. I join them to you, my Lord, who could have saved yourself the pain of "getting involved" with the human race, but you chose instead to save me.

I know there is something greater than myself at work here, and I am ready to embrace it.

It makes me happy to suffer for you, as I am suffering now, and in my own body to do what I can to make up all that has still to be undergone by Christ for the sake of his body, the Church.

Colossians 1:24 (JB)

13

*Jesus Is Taken Down
from the Cross*

*W*e read that at your death there remained a gathering of loyal women. It's not surprising that the women would have stayed; the need to comfort, to clean up, to attend to details seems to be a distinctly, though not exclusively, female trait.

These women were waiting for the chance to do something for you, a service for you and for your memory—to do something for you without someone else objecting or over-ruling. Here you were the powerless one, and they were your caretakers. With the help of Joseph of Arimathea, something good and loving could now be done for you.

Sometimes it's awfully hard to allow others to do for me, Lord. I hate to give up what I think of as "control" of my circumstances, my body, my life. The generous things others do, which they perceive as loving, comforting, and helpful, I sometimes see as controlling, intrusive, and condescending. So often I say, "Oh, I hate to be fussed over!" In saying this, I am really saying that I'm not worth the fussing of others, or that I'm threatened by the very idea of *needing* some help and attention.

Sometimes I'm just so busy trying to control my life and my surroundings that I become blind to another's need to *do for* me, to feel useful. I become too selfish to allow others the chance to perform ministry, to do what is pleasing in God's sight.

The truth is this: on some days I can do for myself, and if I can, I should. But on other days I lack strength, or my will is weak. On those days, I must remember you now, being tended to with the love you so well deserved by people who *needed* to do this small, fussy thing for you, so that they could comfort themselves with the knowledge that they helped.

Help me then, Jesus, to be honest about my limitations and to be understanding and generous when others want to help.

> *Those who love your law have great peace,*
> *and for them there is no stumbling block.*
> Psalm 119:165 (NAB) 1970

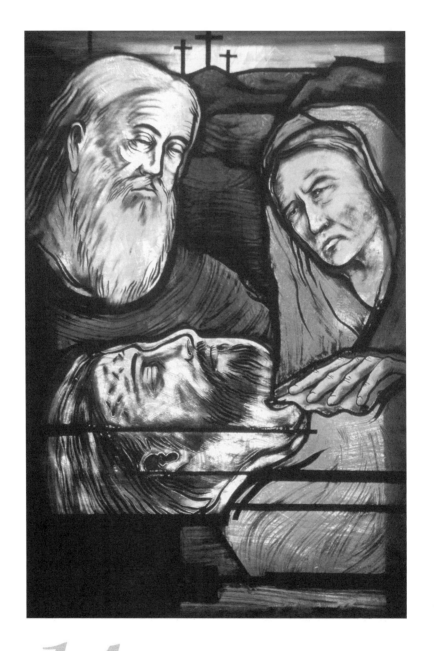

14   *Jesus Is Laid in the Tomb*

*Y*ou were enshrouded and laid in a tomb, and a boulder was rolled in place at the entrance. Closure. Or so they thought.

We know of the glory that followed your entombment, we know that endings are often a state of mind.

In my life I have often thought that something was over, only to discover that something else was merely beginning. I have celebrated getting over illness, rolling stones over the experience, only to find the illness, or its effects, reappearing at a later date. I have addressed hard, painful episodes of my life with honesty and courage, thinking, as I rolled the stone of closure, "I'll never have to deal with *that* again!" But then the memories resurface in dreams or in sudden, paralyzing fears that must once more be soothed down or slain like obstinate dragons.

There are no endings. Things are a continual beginning. Things resurrect. Hope resurrects.

Putting a stone in the way of things may seem to bring closure, but really the stone closes nothing, ends nothing. It just shuts down the comings and goings of the days and times of my life. In his Gospel, Saint Mark tells us that the women who wished to anoint your body wondered, "Who will roll away the stone?"

Lord Jesus, I wish to live without stones and self-placed obstacles. I wish to live without the mindset of closure, which suggests a locking-up and a shutting-out. You are the Christ, the Eternal Daystar. In you there are no shadows. With you, there are no stones required. There are no limits. I will push forward until the stone is cleared away, until it becomes merely the strong rock upon which to rest along the way. I join myself to you now, Lord, as I rise!

My heart is ready, O God, my heart is ready. I will sing, I will sing your praise. Awake, my soul; awake, lyre and harp, I will awake the dawn.

Psalm 57:8-9 (Grail)

O Daystar
O Living Water
O Key of David
O Christ

I praise you for you are my God.
I thank you, for you have heard my plea.

O Man of Jerusalem
  City of Bread,
O Lord of Life
  Saving Cup,

I now walk with you
And each step is illuminated, made new, for
You are the Path of Light.
You are the Wayside Resting Place.
You are the Glory of the City of God.

In your greatness and your compassion,
have mercy on me in my smallness and my humanity.
Bless me as I bless your holy name,
and keep me in your sight,
as I rest a while in you. Amen.